PRAYERS AND FABLES
Meditating on Aesop's Wisdom

PRAYERS AND FABLES
Meditating on Aesop's Wisdom

William Cleary

Sheed & Ward
Kansas City

Also by William Cleary
  Prayers for Lovers
  Prayers To She Who Is
  In God's Presence
  The Lively Garden Prayer Book
  A Doubter's Prayerbook
  Lighten Your Heart
  Churchmouse Tales From the Vatican
  Psalm Services For Group Prayer
  Psalm Services For Church Groups
  Facing God

Sheed & Ward™ is a service of National Catholic Reporter Publishing Company, Inc.

Library of Congress Cataloging-in-Publication Data.
Cleary, William.
    Prayers and fables : meditating on Aesop's wisdom / William Cleary.
        p.   cm.
    Includes index.
    ISBN: 1-55612-960-2 (alk. paper)
    1. Meditations. 2. Prayers. 3. Aesop's fables—Adaptations. 4. Fables, Greek—Adaptations.   I. Aesop's fables.   II. Title.
    BV4832.2.C544   1998
    242—dc21   97-47387
                                                                      CIP

Published by: Sheed & Ward
                      115 E. Armour Blvd.,
                      P.O. Box 419492
                      Kansas City, MO 64141-6492.

To order, call: (800)333-7373

This book is reprinted on recycled paper.

www.natcath.com/sheedward

Cover design by Jane Pitz.

Illustrations by Maureen Noonan.

Contents

III.
Slow and Steady Wins the Day

IV.
History is Written by the Victors

Dedicated
to that cloud of storytellers,
most often mothers or mother-like, God-like, people,
who tiptoe with their listeners
through the wonderworld of stories
wherein happens what is truer than truth.

The very act of storytelling, of arranging memory and invention according to the structure of narrative, is by definition holy. It is a version, however finite, of what the infinite God does. Telling our stories is what saves us; the story is enough. . . .

–James Carroll

Every child, and the child in every one of us, is ready to plead: TELL ME A STORY! For the role of stories is to explain life, and the good stories, in their very substance and in the structure of their language, become revelation. . . .

–Andrew Greeley

Introduction

On Judgment Day, say the Sufis, God will put our heart into a scalepan, and on the other side, a feather. Until they balance, they say, we shall not be allowed into heaven.

Our faith has taught us little in recent years about this—though many of our Saints were lighthearted people: Teresa of Avila, Julian of Norwich, Thomas More, for example—and many others.

Readers would appreciate more focus on this, I believe. It is our long-standing tradition—in contrast to the stereotypical seriousness of theologians and Reformers. How beloved throughout history is the clown, the jokester, the comedian. We need them desperately: they often shake us back to reality, back to humility too, often at great cost to themselves.

The ancient tales of Aesop are full of lightheartedness—a quality Aquinas, following Aristotle, praised as the virtue, *eutrapelia*. Aesop himself, according to our best information, was much more than the entertaining jester whose stories we read to our children. A hunch-back Greek slave with a pronounced speech defect (not unlike Moses), Aesop has blazed like a comet across literary history for 2500 years. Unable to read or write or even speak clearly, he nevertheless has put his personal mark on western civilization forever: the story of the fox and the supposedly sour grapes, of the over-fed hen who stopped laying eggs, of how the tortoise out-raced the hare—will always be a part of our communal imagination.

Plutarch, writing eight centuries after Aesop's death, placed him among his seven wisest men of all time.

Christians might call him more than wise. We will call him holy perhaps—once we take into account the wisdom and discipline involved in the virtue of lightheartedness. For Aquinas *eutrapelia* is serious stuff: a moral virtue, and a quality even of God. (How—but by *eutrapelia*—make sense of critters like the skunk, the dung beetle, or the lightning bug.) A sense of humor is certainly a quality often observed in widely admired human leaders and prophets.

Walking the High Wire. Another quality about Aesop's Fables that is also seldom attended to is that they were all originally told in verse—and only re-telling them in verse begins to capture their peculiar charm and poignancy. The plain facts of any fable are seldom enough to make it aesthetically exciting. It would be like *speaking* the lyrics of a song: a totally different experience than hearing it sung.

Verse—and rhyme—elevate the challenge to the author (the way the high wire elevates the risk at the circus), and therefore add subliminally to the excitement and delight of each fable. Try telling a child the story of hickory dickory dock—in prose lines. It falls flat. If the fables of Aesop you have heard lack eclat for you, try reading them now in verse. There's a world of difference.

The earliest record we have today of Aesop's two hundred-odd fables is found in the writings of the Greek historian Demetrius Phalereus some 300 years after Aesop's death—which was a violent one. Aesop apparently was put to death by the Athenian dictator for accusing the government—through his allegorical story-telling—of criminal injustice. The tale of the hawk and the pigeons (see p. 145) was probably one of his most politically incorrect and offensive fables, and even today would stand as a blistering critique of any dishonest and tyrannical regime.

In the final analysis, Aesop himself is a fable. Born deprived and physically challenged he has managed to profoundly influence the world, filling it with illumination about the human condition, ever so mysterious and baffling. We are all wiser for his lightsome and acrobatic imagination, and for the courage it took to tell his stories full of a wisdom not everyone wanted to hear.

Learning to Pray. To Aesop's unforgettable fables we here add a prayer, often lighthearted itself and occasionally offbeat—only because our Scriptures, from Genesis to Apocalypse, teach us we can talk to our God, and the Abrahamic religions particularly like to use the vehicle of words to make prayer more intelligible—if not ultimately more effectual—than silence.

Most people assume, of course, that speaking to God is allowed and can be helpful. It comes naturally, even when we do not know for sure in just what manner the Divine Mystery hears us. All the Jewish prophets spoke to God in words, often, eloquently, and at great length. The entire Book of Psalms is nothing but words addressed to "the Lord," although I suspect that the real God "in whom we live and move and have our being" (a beautiful God-name from a non-Judeo-Christian philosopher)—grows tired of being called by a name, Lord, that suggests a dominant male person. God is never named that way in this book. See if the names you find here (it is my own interpretive translation) are not more satisfactory. Of course the names you create yourself will be the best.

In the Jewish prophetic tradition, that mysterious healer/teacher Jesus of Nazareth is pictured at prayer just before all the major events in his life: before his baptism, before his 40-day fast, just as his preaching begins, before his first healing, before choosing his major apostles, before his major miracles, before his choice of Peter as leader, before the Sinai vision, before the Last Supper, before he is captured, as he awaits crucifixion, and just before he dies. To speak as if God was listening was second nature to Jesus. The prayers herein follow that lead.

Similarly, as *Prayers and Fables* is pushed from the nest to try its wings as a book, let me ask a special blessing on this work. "Grant, Holy Wisdom, that it be as much fun and as useful to the reader as writing it has been to its author."

Do I hear an "Amen?"

William Cleary
Winter 1998

I.

PEACE OF MIND
IS THE GREATEST WEALTH

1. City Mouse and Country Mouse Exchange Visits

A wealthy city mouse once came
To view his country cousin's clutter,
He stayed for lunch but all they ate
Were sandwiches of peanut butter.

You call that lunch? the rich mouse said,
Call this a house? He laughed with glee,
Come into town tonight, he said,
Step up a notch and visit me!

So in they went and to a house
With walls of stone and gardens green,
And soon were eating steaks and chops
And every kind of haute cuisine.

This is the life! said Country Mouse,
I've been a bumpkin long enough!
THEN suddenly four dogs burst in
With masters shouting, loud and gruff.

LOOK OUT! the city cousin screamed
And dove into a bag of coal,
The country mouse leaped to the floor
And ran like lightning down a hole,

And never stopped until he came
Back to his peaceful country door.
Enough! he said, *of city life,*
It's great—but not worth dying for.

Moral: Peace of mind
is the greatest wealth.

3

Prayer for Peace of Mind

My first prayer, Loving Spirit, is always for peace of
mind,
that abiding tranquillity I observe in my most admired
heroines and heroes:
Etty Hillesum, Thomas Merton, Flannery O'Connor,
Gandhi.

I am ready to face serenely
all the sources of disquiet in my soul,
and especially the envy I feel for the rich, the gifted and
the lucky.

Oh, I would enjoy having the virtuosity of Oprah
Winfrey
or the wide-ranging intelligence of Stephen Jay Gould,
but I value the gifts I have
even though they have failed to make me rich.

Your way with me, Mysterious Spirit,
has been generous in the extreme
and supportive beyond all my dreams.

And if, before I die, a little luck comes my way, see:
with this virtuous attitude I have,
it would do me no harm.
Amen.

From Psalm 119

Blest are they whose way is blameless,
    who walk in your light,
Blest are they who know your guidance,
    who seek for you with all their heart.

Your strong voice guides my footsteps,
    I stay securely on your paths.
Grant us skill to wait and listen
    so we will always hear your voice.

Look kindly on your faithful servant,
    Keep me reverent of your words.
Open up my eyes that I may appreciate
    the wonders of your way. . . .

2. The Bald Knight Laughs At Himself

There once was a knight, courageous and bold,
Who lost all his hair as he grew old,
So rather than blush, he bought instead
A thick black wig for the top of his head.
    One day as he heard his doorbell chime
    He tried on his wig for the very first time
    But as he saluted a lady friend,
    A heartless wind came round the bend.

"Whoosh" went his wig up into the air
And quick as a flash his head was bare!
Up went his eyebows, down went his jaw!
The lady friend squelched a loud guffaw,
    She pulled out a hanky to cover her face
    But squeals came giggling through the lace,
    She stuffed her bonnet into her teeth
    But snickers snuck out underneath.

Then, lo, the knight's own laugh broke through,
And he grabbed his belly and doubled in two,
Till tears rolled down his aging face
And chuckles poured out like a holy grace.

Finally the knight spoke after a pause:
I have to admit—how silly I was!
How could I hope false hair would stay
When even my real hair blew away?
    The friend then smiled—and hugged the one
    Whose laugh at himself contained such fun.

Moral: Nothing is quite so laughable
as our own vanity.

Prayer to Take One's Self Lightly

Amazing God,
you have given me lots of reasons to laugh at myself
especially when I catch a glimpse of my soul's costume:
a clown's battered hat
(affecting nobility),
a smile-marked mouth
(hiding the melancholy within)
and my oversize shoes
(suggesting a world-shaking agenda).

Add to that my comic pomposity,
my transparent pretensions to wisdom,
and my bumbling pratfalls en route to success at last.

Why am I slow to laugh at myself, so slow to dance,
so concerned about how I look?

Bless the clown in me,
Thou Captivated Audience for all you've created.
Give me laughter, dance and song
to lighten the burdens I carry
and soften the sharp edges of my self
that others around me feel.
Amen.

From Psalm 98

Sing a new song in the House of God
    for the wonders of earth abound.
The marvels of God's mysterious ways
    call forth a Day of Joy.

Our God wins love and reverent praise
    from every part of the globe,
God's fairness toward all the creatures on earth
    means justice will long be praised.

Sing joyfully, all you continents
    break into festive song,
Take up the harp to give praise to God
    with songs of sweetest sound. . . .

3. A Man Is Undone By Two Loving Wives

There once was a time, very long, long ago,
    When a man with *two* wives was thought bolder,
So one middle-aged fellow whose hair was half grey
    Married two wives, one young and one older.

The younger thought Hubby should always look young,
    So she'd pull out grey hairs from his head,
But the older wife wanted a mate her own age,
    So she'd snatch out the black hairs instead.

Of course he was flattered they loved him so much
    And rejoiced he was *multiply* wed
Till one morning he looked in the mirror to find
    There was NOT ONE HAIR left on his head.

Moral: Wanting too much
can leave one empty-handed.

Prayer for Healthy Self-Esteem

Let me look at myself for a moment through the eyes of
your creating Love.
Do you see me as a mother might?
as a father might, or a brother or sister, or true friend?
As an admirer might?

If I encircle myself with all of these,
then double in each their capacity to care,
then triple it, then raise it to infinity,
I have some glimpse of the circle of love with which
you, Loving Mystery,
care for me.
Need I multiply admirers to convince my heart I am
lovable?

While your creation is drenched in beauty
and held together by a magnetism stretching to the ends
of all that is,
still I am in your eyes strikingly beautiful,
and your longing for me and my wellbeing
goes beyond the ends of all that is.

Grace me, then, with an inkling of your love
whenever my self-esteem flags.
Your view is the truth: Hozanna.
Amen.

From Psalm 25

My God, in You I trust,
    let me never be put to shame
    let not my enemies exult over me.

Make me to know your ways, Holy One
    teach me your paths,
Lead me in your truth, and teach me
    for You are the God of my life.

For You I wait all the day long,
Be mindful of your mercy, O God,
    and of your steadfast love
    for they have been my life from of old. . . .

4. The Peace-Loving Sun Defeats the Wind

The Wind and Sun were arguing
Which was the best at everything.
Let's test, said Wind, *If you or I
Can make men take off coat and tie.*
    So Wind blew strong with snow and hail
    Till one man's coat flapped like a sail
    But he resisted all the more
    And pulled it tighter than before.

How foolish, said the noble Sun:
Now watch who'll be the winning one.
And he sent sunbeams so extreme
That all the lakes showed puffs of steam,
    And that man such discomfort felt
    That his defense began to melt!
    He tore off tie and coat and shirt
    And dropped them gladly in the dirt.

So ever since we've learned, of course,
Persuasion's BETTER FAR than force.

Moral: Force can never accomplish
what persuasion can.

Prayer Not to Be Mortal

Holy Life-Giving Spirit,
inhabiting and energizing every part of this world and
every world,
you must—amazingly—have time and caringness
enough
to pay attention to me and my small needs
for I am your beloved invention, your child,
and you have an infinity of time at your disposal.

Today I must ask for the impossible:
first, never to be ill, and second, never to die.
I know the first is virtually impossible
and the second utterly impossible,
yet my heart cries out for health and life—
and always will.
My heart prays for this regardless of my better judgment.

Hope perches in my soul and "sings the tune without
the words,
and never stops at all."

Of course you will ignore these prayers.
You are not persuaded to answer them as I desire.
Or perhaps you will answer them in a way I don't
expect,
some way wrapt in mystery.
Certainly pressure doesn't work with you: fasting,
sacrifices, or long prayers.

God of mystery, you are God.
May your way prevail
and your wise caringness surround us always
on this worrisome road toward immortality.
Amen.

From Psalm 16

Preserve me, O God, for in you I take refuge,
I say to my God, You are my heart's home,
    I have no rest apart from you.
    My God, my chosen portion and my cup,
    Your love and care mean everything to me

In the night also my heart instructs me
and I find You, God, right there before my eyes.
    Because you hold my hand, I shall not fear
    Therefore my heart is glad, and my soul rejoices,
    My body also dwells safe and secure.

For you point out to me the path of life,
And in your presence there is a richness of joy.
    Preserve me, O God, for in you I take refuge.
    I say to my God, You are my heart's home. . . .

5. An Astrologer Suffers a Foolish Accident

One famous Astrologer studied the stars,
    So he could the future foretell!
With his eyes on the sky he went walking one night
    And by accident fell down a well.

He shouted and screamed till a farmer nearby
    Pulled him out—but reviled his conceit,
Pray tell, said the farmer, *why pry into stars*
    But lose track of what's under your feet?

Moral: In flights of abstraction,
watch your step.

Prayer Against Abstractions

With your help, Creator Mystery,
I will try to maintain a balance in my life
between book knowledge
and the knowledge I have from experience.

You are not an abstraction.
You are a Mother and a Father and a Companion to me,
and for that I give profound thanks: be near.

Wash from my mind
the illusion that dusty abstractions and theories
contain the most important truth—
while I overlook the feelings of my friends,
the faces of anguished children,
the pollution in the air I breathe,
the threat of nuclear annihilation,
the orange magic of the sunset, promising good
weather.

Grace me with a sense of your real, not theoretical,
presence,
so that along with star-gazing explorations in my head,
I may keep my feet solidly in the real world,
imperiled, hurting,
charged with your grandeur.
Amen.

From Psalm 29

The voice of the Spirit is upon the earth's waters,
    the God of glory thunders,
The voice of the Spirit is awesome,
    the voice of God is full of majesty.

The voice of the Spirit splits the cedars,
    God's voice breaks the great trees of Lebanon,
It is God who makes Lebanon to skip like a calf
    and Sirion run like a wild young ox.

The cry of God shakes the wilderness,
    our God shakes the wilderness of Kadesh
    The voice of the Spirit makes the oaks to whirl
    and strips the forests bare. . . .

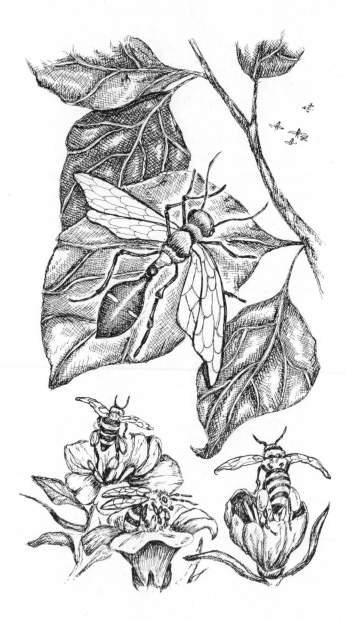

6. The Wise Wasp Uncovers the Truth

Some bees built their honeycomb high in a tree,
    But the drones claimed *they'd* made the comb too,
So they all asked a Wasp who was wonderfully wise
    If she'd judge what was false and what true.

That's easy, said Wasp, *Each make a new comb*
    And we'll see if it's equally sweet.
OKAY! said the bees.   *OH, NO!* said the drones.
    The Wasp smiled—for her task was complete.

Moral: Claims are best tested
by deeds.

Prayer for Honesty

God Creator of the evolving human race,
why are we so peculiarly hungry
for credit for what we have done,
that we are even inclined to accept praise that is not
due us?

Unless we are cautious, we quickly exaggerate our
successes
and adroitly cover up our failures.
forgetting that before your eyes we never need pretend
for we are transcendently beautiful.

We ask you for the sweet grace of forthright honesty:
to have the heart to appreciate the sublime beauty
of the truth
and the ugliness of all falsehood,
to be in the future even painfully honest when
necessary.

In fact, if we promise complete candor from this day
forward,
could you exempt us, merciful God,
from ever confessing
those few little exaggerations we may have been guilty
of in the past?
Amen.

From Psalm 103

God is full of mercy and generosity,
forgiving and full of care,
God does not deal with us according to our sins,
nor repay us according to our failues.

For as the sky is high above the earth,
so great does God's love tower over us.
And as far as east is from the west,
so far does God remove our sins from us.

As parents pity their own children,
so God has pity on the faithful.
Bless your God, O my soul,
and let all that is within me bless God's holy name. . . .

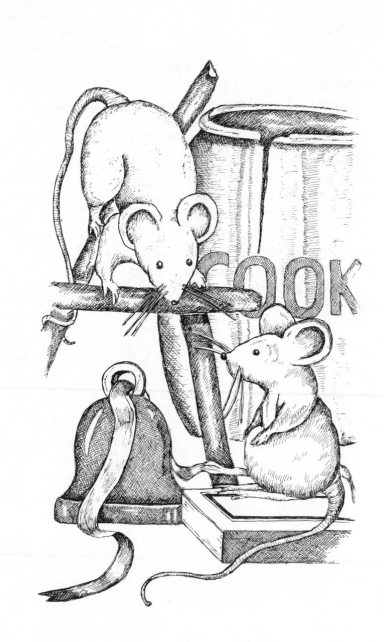

7. The Little Mice Plan to Bell the Cat

Believe me, said a youthful mouse,
  That cat makes too much fuss,
The silly thing just sits and waits
  To capture one of us.

You're right, a peer said, looking grim,
  I find the cat disgusting,
You never know just where she is!
  No wonder we're mistrusting.

Quickly a committee formed
  And came up with an answer!
A bell around the kitty's neck
  Would neutralize the cancer!

The crowd rejoiced: *OUR PROBLEM'S SOLVED!*
But Grandma Mouse looked leery,
She sighed a tired sigh and said:
I've just one simple query.
  Who'll be the one to volunteer
  To go and bell the kitty?
And all kept perfect silence then,
Especially the committee.

Moral: Many a plan has just one flaw:
  no one has the courage to try it.

Prayer for Courage

Audacious Creator,
all our words to you or about you fall short.
How shall we fit ourselves into your world?

Too often you seem to terrify and perplex us.
Then, when we need you most, it's as if you don't exist.

You appear indescribably full of daring
to invent for us a world
that seems so unsatisfactory to human needs—
and yet a creation awesomely rich in gratuitous beauty
and in incomprehensible vastness and complexity.

Give us the wisdom to stay connected to the earth,
despite its mysteriousness.
Give us the realism not to expect miracles of ourselves.
But fill our hearts with courage now and then
to do what must and should be done,
despite the danger.
Amen.

From Psalm 130

Out of the depths I cry to you, O God,
    O God, hear my voice.
    Let your ears be attentive
        to my voice in supplication.

If you will count our failures, Holy One,
    who can stand?
    But You are rich in mercy:
        this we revere.

We trust in you, Creator,
    and your covenant.
    We are more full of hope
        than sentinels awaiting dawn. . . .

8. The Thirsty Crow Gets Good Advice

The crow flew down, near dead with thirst,
The land below with drought was cursed,
    And animals began to die
    Because no rain fell from the sky.

Then that poor crow a pitcher found
Half-full of water on the ground.
    He stretched as far as he could bear,
    But could not reach the water there.

Alas, he cried, *My neck is sore,*
I cannot stretch it any more,
And if the pitcher I should break
The earth will all my water take!

An owl nearby began to shout:
Put pebbles in that pitcher's spout
To raise the water to the brink,
THEN you reach in and take a drink!

It worked! He drank till he was through
And lived to crow about it too,
    And learned that day it's wise indeed
    To get advice when you're in need.

Moral: Answers to great problems often come
from unexpected sources.

Prayer of Thanks for the Scriptures

Spirit Creator and Source of All,
I give thanks for the wisdom of the Bible and ask to live
in its light.

It is full of refreshment for me
since in its pages I learn that I am wealthy
beyond my wildest dreams,
surrounded by an ocean of love,
utterly sure of your support tomorrow
with a dozen opportunities today
for the joys of friendship, meaning and human solidarity.
I thank you for my blessings.

We hear of multi-millionnaire brothers and sisters
who live without trusted friends,
who feel surrounded by enemies
and are suspicious of every kindly greeting:
save them in your mercy.

They may have servants, mansions, investments,
and money pouring in each month
but facing the eye of the needle,
they may be destitute of hope,
and deprived of your presence shining in the least of
the brethren.

Give me a heart of gratitude for my own lot, Holy Spirit,
and a heart of sympathy for all those with less.
Amen.

From Psalm 85

We hear God's voice from the highest hill:
As the poor cry out for peace.
>Help is near when we turn to God,
>and worship and justice increase.

Kindness and truth shall meet as friends,
And justice and peace shall kiss.
>Truth shall spring from the fertile earth,
>and compassion fill every abyss.

Look, God comes with a wealth of gifts,
Our faces shall turn to the light,
>Justice shall bloom where God has walked
>and mercy sprout up overnight. . . .

9. The Canny Dog Out-Smarts the Thief

A thief crept close to a house one night
Where a canny dog stood guard,
The dog smelled meat!—It was tossed by the thief
As he tiptoed through the yard.

"BEGONE! *You contemptible thief!"* barked the dog,
And the crook turned and ran, full of fright.
He looked like a thief, said the canny dog,
And his gifts made me SURE I was right!

Moral: Always be suspicious
of an overly generous gift.

Prayer Not to Be Narrow-Minded

I ask you, Intimate Mystery,
that in my hesitating distrust of unfamiliar spiritualities,
I not become narrow-minded.

To be simplistically judgmental comes so naturally
to those who are privileged.
We assume that our high level of civility
has nothing to do with our unearned advantages,
and we condemn out of hand those with other priorities.

Make me wary of a scoffing mentality
that flatters my own ego,
while always assuming for myself
the high moral ground.

Holy Wisdom, seeing the truth of everything,
share with me the light of genuine faith
that I may judge more justly
and live more tolerantly and honestly.
Amen.

After Psalm 34

This day I bless the God of all
    who knows my sorrow and my fear,
    yet in my solitary agony,
    I still could say: My God is here.

So turn to God with radiant face,
    Let praise and courage be your prayer,
    Rejoice in this blest human family:
        when we seek God, our God is there. . . .

10. The Wounded Wolf Calls for Help

A wolf lying wounded, all haggard and pale,
Saw a sheep walking by looking hardy and hale,
Dear Sheep! cried the wolf, *Do you see how I bleed?*
Just a wee bit of water is all that I need,
> *If you just bring me drink, I'll regain all my health,*
> *Then later find something to eat by myself.*

Answered Sheep, *If I bring you some water to drink,*
I'll be bringing you dinner as well too, I think.
You'll eat up MYSELF, that's the thing that you'll do!
So I shall reject this petition from you,
> *Though my heart may go out and feel true sympathy,*
> *You don't have the mercy you're asking of me!*

Moral: Always be slow
to trust the powerful.

Prayer for the Over-Empowered

God, Spirit of Justice,
whose every holy word to us urges compassion
for those suffering from unfairness and injustice,
give us eyes to see unfair over-empowerment wherever
it is hidden:
where skin color alone or gender alone confers
privileges,
where inheritance alone gives presumed virtue,
where special talents of mind and body
—meant to bless a whole group—
are hoarded for individual gain.

With your help we shall learn to value solidarity over
domination,
justice over privilege,
and experience both the immense energies hidden in
diversity,
and the enlightenment that comes with mutual regard.
Amen.

From Psalm 85

Who is like God our God
  Who is seated in the heavens,
Who looks far down upon the skies and the earth,
  Who fills the earth with justice?

God raises the poor from the dust,
  And lifts the needy from the ash heap,
To make them sit with princes,
  With the very princes of the earth.

God gives the barren woman a home,
  Making her the joyous mother of children.
Bless God, O servants of God,
  Praise God's holy name. . . .

II.

THE HEART MAKES MORE DECISIONS THAN THE HEAD

11. The Comedian Out-Squeals a Pig

There once was a king who offered a prize
    To the best pig-like sound anyone could devise,
So a well-known comedian there in the place
    Stepped up on the stage with a grin on his face.

The people were laughing before he began,
    And they screamed when he walked like a bow-legged man,
Then he covered his head as he took a big breath
    And he squealed like a pig being tortured to death.

Now there in the crowd stood a hick with a pig
    So he hid it inside where his jacket was big,
And he crawled on the stage and then twisted its ear,
    And the sound of that pig was amazing to hear.

BEGONE! said the crowd, *You don't need to pretend,*
    You can't make a pig sound to save your rear end!
So the hick showed his pig, but the king hollered *NAY!*
    You lose! That comedian triumphs today!

Moral: The heart makes
more decisions
than the head.

Prayer to Like the Person I See in the Mirror

Dear Sacred Lifegiver, my God,
look in the mirror with me.
I am wise enough to understand that what I see is
beautiful,
but I want to believe it too.
I want my heart to follow my mind.

What you see there, O God, is what I am.
What I see there is the mystery of my identity
hidden behind a mask
scored by laughter, hurt and questioning,
but still essentially shaped as it was
when emerging from my mother's womb,
eyes unopened, face pink and desperate.

In my ordinary somnolent state of mind
I disbelieve in my own beauty
in favor of what my wounded heart has somehow
decided:
I am worthless.
Wake me up to the sunrise of my own value.

I thank you for what I am today, Holy Wisdom,
for what I am learning to see in the mirror.
And give me the enlightenment to enjoy the sight
as much as you do.
Amen.

After Psalm 25

Guide me in just ways, O God, My God,
    teach me the paths of honesty and light,
for your good help I wait all the day long,
    Come lead me on and show me what is right.

Our God is generous to all the crushed,
    And helps the heavy-burdened ones to cope,
God helps all humble seekers find the truth,
    and shows the poor how they may live in hope. . . .

I so adore the sound you make!
A silly donkey said one day
In talking to some grasshoppers
Whom he found singing in the hay.

My wildest dream would be to sing
Like holy cherubim on high!
What do you eat that helps you sing
So like the angels in the sky?

You'll be amazed at what we eat:
NOTHING BUT DEW! the critters said,
So Donkey tried that diet too—
And in a short time he was dead.

Moral: Envy can make
fools of us.

Prayer for Inspired Music

Holy Inventor of exploding lightning and howling storm,
birdsong and wolf call,
pounding wave and sighing breeze,
of ten thousand patterns of rhythm pulsing everywhere,
and of all nature's strings and reeds, brasses and skins
in which we discover sound,
give us the music that can make life more possible,
love more unforgettable,
and courage grow in our hearts.

Is there not a harmony deep in the fabric of things?
Musicians make this leap of faith,
and even a faintly heard chord of this harmony
makes would-be musicians of us all.

Cure the despair that shrieks in the din of noise.
Hum in the creative ear of the insightful,
the compassionate
and the valiant—
so that they, in their inspired architecture of sound,
will build cathedrals resonant with your truth and
beauty.
Amen.

From Psalm 96

Sing to God a new song,
    Sing to God, all the earth,
Sing to God, bless God's name,
    Tell of God's rescue from day to day.

Declare God's glory among the nations,
    God's marvelous works among all the peoples,
For great is God, and greatly to be praised,
    Greatly to be honored above all gods.

Let the sky be glad, and the earth rejoice,
    Let the sea roar, and all that fills it,
Let the fields exult with everything that grows.
    Then all the trees of the forest shall sing for joy. . . .

A hungry old fox spotted grapes one night
And the bunches looked juicy and long,
     The vines hung high
     In the midnight sky
And the scent of the fruit was strong.

HOORAY! he said, *What a perfect dessert!*
So he hunched down low to prepare,
     Then with all of his might
     He leaped that height—
But his jaws snapped down on air.

He leaped again, then he leaped, and leaped,
But his teeth never touched the prize,
     And his back was hurt
     Where he'd hit the dirt,
And he'd anger and tears in his eyes.

So at last, worn out and sick at heart,
He went home to his cozy bower,
     Who cares? he said
     As he lay down his head,
Those silly grapes were sour!

Moral: It is easy to scorn
that which we ourselves
cannot attain.

Prayer in Defeat

Look with me, Mothering Spirit, Provident Father,
through all the windows of the past, one by one,
and see as I do those visions of life passages
where I emerged hurt, shamed, and defeated.

See, there and there, how I wanted to die?
See the triumphant grin on my opponent's face?
See my heart cast down by rejection,
down into the dust, into the earth, into the swamp?

See how they misjudged me,
not taking into account the heavy burdens I struggled
under,
never paying attention to the heart
that so passionately yearned for success
but failed to reach it?

See how unfair it all was:
they so undeservedly rich,
me so inexplicably poor?

O Spirit All-comforting, Parent All-Provident,
Holy and Loving Presence,
drain from these visions—as much as you can—
all that is sour and unredeemable.
Teach me to find comfort in your love.
Pour on my turbulent soul your oil of gladness.
Amen.

From Psalm 40

Do not, O God, withhold your mercy from me,
    your faithful servant.
Let your steadfast love and your faithfulness
    ever keep me safe.

For evils without number have encircled me,
    My troubles surround me till I hardly can see,
They are more numerous than the hairs of my head.
    My heart almost fails in my anguish.

For behold, I am poor, I am needy—
    but the God I trust takes thought for me.
You are my help and deliverer.
    do not tarry, my God and my Hope. . . .

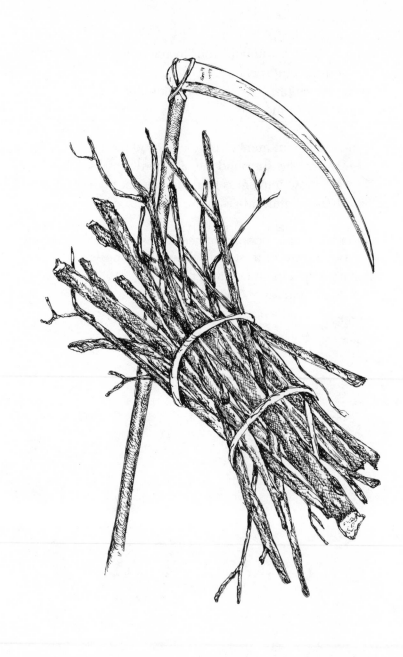

14. A Ghost Cures an Old Man's Despair

The weary old man had traveled far
With a great pack of wood on his back,
His bones cried out and his feet were sore
And his mood was dreary and black.

In despair he threw down his burden of wood,
COME, DEATH! he groaned to the skies,
And suddenly Death stood there by his side,
Smiling and holding a scythe.

What is it? said Death, *Can I be of help?*
But the old man was stunned to the core,
O please, said he, *I've just one wish:*
Help me pick up this pack once more.

Moral: It is one thing to think about death,
and another to see it really coming.

Prayer Against Despair

God of Surprises,
surrounding me with your love and energy
even when I seem to be
totally alone,
Ocean of Possibilities as multiple as the swirl-shapes of
waves worldwide,
or the sunlight refractions from seaside sand,
I need your dynamic presence in my heart just now
to drive away the despair and sadness
that have welled up so high within me
that it feels as if I'm going under.

With your help I can carry on under this burden
till the clock ticks awhile and the clouds disappear over
the horizon
—as they always do—
and sweet shalom returns to my soul.

Live in me now, Holy One,
as one more mystery works itself out
deep within me,
and your revelation unfolds in my heart.
Amen.

From Psalm 69

Save me, O God,
    For I am near drowning,
I sink in the quicksand
    where there is no foothold,
I have come into deep waters
    and the waves sweep over me.

I am weary with crying,
    my throat is parched,
My eyes grow dim with waiting:
    More in number than the hairs of my head are my
    enemies.

O God, You know my folly
    the wrongs I have done are not hidden from You
Let not those who hope in You be put to shame
    O Holy God of mulitudes. . . .

15. A Farmer Kills the Goose Who Lays Golden Eggs

A lucky farmer had a goose
That every single day
Would lay one perfect golden egg,
And hide it in the hay.

Each day the farmer found the egg
And took it to the town
And got good money for his egg
And grew in wide renown.

It's not enough, the farmer said,
I think I do surmise
That goose has pounds of gold inside
Just judging from his size.

He killed the goose and looked within
That goose's guts and fuzz,
But nothing did he find at all
Except—how DUMB he was.

Moral: Don't let the perfect
destroy the good.

However you bring it about,
God Most Knowledgeable, Most Intelligent, Most Wise,
can you help me to win something like $5 million
for a $1 investment?
If I speak to you humbly, respectfully, and frequently—
will you hear my prayer?
I would be wildly generous with my money if I win,
and I would donate to all the major religious causes.

I am not saying I am "worthy" of winning,
but then who is?

I would just be eternally grateful.   ·
And most of my major problems would be solved
so I'd have more time for church, for volunteer work
and private meditation.

So bless me with luck if you can.
Or curse me with luck: whatever.
Just make me lucky, Holy God,
however you bring it about.
Amen.

From Psalm 26

Stand by me, Faithful Spirit,
    For I have walked in faithfulness,
Stand by me, God of my heart,
    I have trusted you without wavering.

Test me, Holy One, and try me,
    Test my heart and test my mind,
For your steadfast love is before my eyes
    And I walk in faithfulness. . . .

16. The Camel Copies the Monkey

One day when all the beasts sat down
To have a meal in jungle town,
    One monkey pranced and clowned
Till all the creatures came to see
And cheered her with ecstatic glee
    To watch her dance around.

At the applause a camel stood,
Annoyed the monkey was so good,
    And took a dancing leap
Up in the air with feet kicked high,
And snapped her teeth and winked her eye,
    Then landed in a heap.

Camel, BEGONE! The beasts did shout
And took a stick and drove her out
    And sent her on her way,
Then brushed their hands and preened their fur,
So glad to be relieved of her
    Preposterous display.

Moral: Longing for applause
only makes you do
ridiculous things.

Holy Heart at the center of everything, loving me,
Holy Strength, creating and holding together all that is,
Holy Eyes, seeing my plain self exactly as I am,
do you enjoy the clownish movements of my personal
soul?

Do you observe how I would love to associate with the
likes of Mother Teresa,
be famous for conspicuous heroism, be revered
worldwide?
How I would enjoy being pursued
for my opinion about everything?
How much fun it would be
to have a mountain of spectacular accomplishments
in my resume?

No, don't answer these unspoken prayers
from my false heart.
Instead, Holy Wisdom, keep doing what you're doing:
creating me,
caring about me,
enjoying me.
Amen.

From Psalm 25

My God, in you I put my trust,
    I shall never be dishonered or disgraced,
My enemies shall never win out over me,
    I shall never despair.

Help me always to know your ways, my God,
    Teach me your paths.
Guide me along the way of truth,
    And lead me not into illusion.

For you are the Shepherd of all my ways
    And the hope of all my dreams.
For you I wait all the day long,
    Keeping watch all my days. . . .

A mouse, lean and hungry, squeezed into a box
Full of barley and ate like a pig,
Then he tried to get out—but the hole was too small
For a mouse with a stomach so big.

HELP! HELP! screamed the mouse at a weasel nearby,
But the weasel said, *Wait awhile, sir,*
You can only accomplish such difficult things
When you're hungry and lean like you were.

Moral: There are some things
only hungry people
can accomplish.

Prayer for Self-Knowledge

Despite my training and experience, God of Wisdom,
I know I walk in profound ignorance.
Though I once was ravenous for knowledge,
too little of that childlikeness remains.

Not only does the world around me escape my
understanding,
but also my own heart is far too little known by me.
I lose my center, take on too much baggage, hunger for
the wrong thing.

Though I sometimes walk in prayer and mindfulness
still I remain, with the Apocalypse fool,
"wretched, pitiable, poor, blind and naked."

Give me a sense of humor about myself, Holy One,
and a ready honesty to recognize—and forgive—
my own illusions and self-centeredness.

Let me accept myself as you, Loving Mystery, accept me
and after the passage of time,
perhaps I can revive the wholesome energies of a
childlike heart.
Amen.

From Psalm 13

How long, dear God, how long?
    Could it be you are forgetting me?
    Could it be you hide your face from me?
How long must I feel this pain,
    and have sorrow at heart all the day?
How long shall heart-sickness invade me and rule
    over me?

Consider, O God, and answer.
Enlighten my vision, dear God, my God,
    lest I sleep the sleep of death,
    lest my enemies say, "We have won the victory!"
    lest my foes rejoice because I am shaken.

But I shall have trusted your steadfast love,
    and my heart shall rejoice at your rescue,
Then I will sing my song to you
    because You have been my God. . . .

18. The Hunter Condemns a Traitorous Partridge

A hunter caught a partridge one fine day,
And the partridge screamed: *Friend! let me get away*
And I'll become your decoy and your slave
So you'll catch all the partridges that you crave!

YOU VILLAIN! said the hunter, *Now you'll die*
For not just one but two good reasons why.
The first: you are my favorite "recipe,"
And second: punishment for treachery.

Moral: Once we betray our friend
to save ourselves,
only a fool would trust us
in anything.

Prayer for Loyalty

Creating Mystery,
caring for me like a perfect mother,
present to me like a doting and proud father,
full of love,
give me the inner firmness of a loyal heart—
which will bind me
into communion with you and with my life companions.

Whenever I see your purposes at stake,
give me the grace to champion your cause all I can.

Grace me with loyalty to all I am close to,
and no less to all your desires
for justice, connectedness and creativity
in the world.
Amen.

From Psalm 91

O God, You are my refuge, they will say,
    all who dwell in the shelter of the Most High,
    who abide in the shadow of the All Compassionate One.
My God, You are my fortress, they will say,
    You are the One in whom I trust.

God's strength protects me always from despair,
    and under holy wings I will find refuge.
God's faithfulness is shield and armor,
    I never shall be abandoned. . . .

19. The Sun Plans a Wedding

Once upon a summer's noon
A parrot spread the news that soon
    There'd be a glorious wedding of the Sun!
What joy! said Pig, *What ecstasy!*
I'll dance a jig! he said in glee,
    And all the other creatures joined the fun.

Until an aged Toad said, *WAIT!*
Have you reflected on our fate
    If we get much more heat around these parts?
Suppose when wedding bells are done
Are born ten children of the sun?
    We'd have ten times the heat he now imparts!
    A thing that some call ecstasy
    For others may be tragedy,
        So much of life depends upon your plight!

The ancient toad then looked around:
The pig was staring at the ground,
    And all the creatures nodded he was right.

Moral: Happy occasions for some
can be devastating events
for others.

Prayer for the Common Good

Your way is best, Holy Mystery,
however you have arranged the events of my life.
Help me to reject all competition with others,
all judgment of their souls,
and all yearning for special good fortune for myself.

May the common good, not my own good, be my
principal concern.
Make me especially concerned for the good of the
oppressed,
that they may have their share of human joy.

May my heart long for justice most of all,
that no one be left out,
that no one be pre-judged,
and no one be without the essentials of a good life:
warm shelter, proper food, health care, education
and the respect due to every part of the holy web of
life.
Amen.

After Psalm 95

If today you hear the voice of God,
    harden not your heart, but be aware,
And turn your face to those who are in need:
    the voice and cry and call of God is there.

Come, bow before the source of every life,
    Come, kneel before the graciousness of God,
For Earth's Creator is a caring guide
    Who shepherds us with loving staff and rod.

Come, sing together joy before our God,
    And greet our Rock of life and love and peace,
Seek for the face of God with songs of thanks,
    The God who makes our life grow and increase. . . .

20. The Bragging Candle Learns a Lesson

One night a candle glimmered bright,
And brilliantly sent forth his light
    And beams around him spread,
Behold, I'm brighter than the sun
And moon and stars all heaped as one!
    The bragging candle said.

Just then a wind (from heaven, no doubt)
Blew down and snuffed the candle out,
    And darkness filled the night
Till someone lit the candle's wick
And said, *Be modest now, not thick:*
    No wind will ever snuff out HEAVEN'S light.

Moral: Puffed up egotism
is quickly deflated.

Prayer Not to Shame Others

Holy Mystery,
sole spectator before the turbulent oceans of feelings
that are the secret inner life of your human creations
(for you see our hearts),
give us the wisdom to live peacefully with each other
without the pain of colliding egos and competitive
shaming.

Teach us how not to fear and envy each other,
how to eschew competition in favor of deference and
cooperation,
how to be so aware of the sensitivities of others
that their feelings are always our concern.

Make us each a fountain of refreshment to those we
encounter,
alert to the dangerous power we have to shame and
humiliate others,
the pain of which is excruciating.

Instead help us to empower and invigorate
each person we meet.
Amen.

From Psalm 40

I have waited for God with patient heart,
    and God bend down and heard my cry,
And sent a song into my mouth,
    a joyous song of thanks and praise.

You did never desire burnt sacrifice,
    but you gave me instead a listening heart,
Oblations and gifts you never asked.
    Then I uttered the words: Behold I come!

In the front of the book they wrote of me:
    to do your will, it is my joy!
And all you ask, my living God,
    shall be a law within my heart. . . .

III.

SLOW AND STEADY WINS THE DAY

21. The Tortoise Outraces the Hare

One day a young hare who almost could fly
Began to make fun when a tortoise crept by:
>   *How slowly you walk! Are you 90 years old?*
>   *You're slow as molasses left out in the cold.*
The tortoise looked up with a smile on his face,
Mister Hare, said the Tortoise, *Would you care to race?*
>   *What? Race with a tortoise?* said Hare in disgust,
>   *I can run like the wind and leave you in the dust!*

Said the owl: *Let's try it! We'll all come to see*
If Hare or if Tortoise the swifter one be!
>   *Tomorrow we'll gather along the deer track*
>   *And the race will go down to the river and back.*
Next morning the owl gave a hoot as a sign
And the racers took off in the glistening sunshine,
>   The hare ran halfway and was laughing and crowing
>   While poor little tortoise was still getting going.

Some riverside flowers attracted the hare
So he had quite a mouthful but he didn't care.
>   Although he got sleepy, he thought: *I can rest*
>   *And still come in first in this silly contest.*
But as he was snoozing that tortoise slipped by
Like a slow-motion cloud in the summertime sky,
>   And laughter exploded when that hare awoke,
>   To find not the tortoise but HE was the joke.

Moral: Slow and steady
wins the day.

Prayer for Humility

So many of us, Creator Spirit,
live in an illusory world.
Like the hare, we can be presumptuous and arrogant.
Unlike the tortoise, we want the odds on our side.

Give us the illumination that comes with humility and
courage.

So often our pride and arrogance
grow out of gifts we received gratuitously,
with no deserts on our side at all.
So often our despair is the fruit of illusory expectations
of ourselves
and failure to acknowledge you in whom we live and
move and have our being.

There is wisdom in knowing and admitting the truth:
all we have and are comes from you.
That enlightenment is already an unexpected victory.
Amen.

From Psalm 39

I spoke: Dear God, let me know my end,
 and what is the measure of my days,
let me comprehend how fleeting my life is.

Behold, You have made my days very short,
 and my lifetime is as nothing in your sight,
Surely all of us exist as a mere breath,
 Surely a human goes about as a shadow. . .

And now, My God, for what do I wait?
 My hope is in You alone,
Hear my prayer, O God,
 and give ear to my cry.

Do not remain silent when I weep
 for I am but a passing guest in this place,
 a traveler, like all my forebears. . . .

An oak, torn up by a typhoon,
Went floating down a river soon—
    Where reeds grew lithe and tall.
Astonished, Oak called to a reed,
You must be powerful indeed
    To live through such a squall!

Oh, no, said Reed, *It isn't power*
That helps us hour after hour
    To live through wind and blast,
You foolish oak, you fought the wind!
Were you less stiff and disciplined,
    You'd not fall down so fast.

    From centuries of wind and chance
    We've learned to bend and yield and dance,
        Pretending not to strive,
    So— diplomatic to the core—
    We lose some fights, but win the war,
        And in the end survive.

Moral: It's better to bend the rules a little
    when they begin to stifle life.

Prayer to Fear God Less

Holy God who constantly eludes us,
after 3,000 years of thinking of you as a Lord,
a dominant, solitary, male divinity,
it is not surprising we find ourselves in a rut.

We humans fashion you from our most dreaded earthly
models—
authoritarian earthly male royalty—,
and thereafter the very thought of you as a Lord
oppresses us—
as such royalty usually does on earth.

You are really not a God of commandments,
though such a God may have been helpful
when he was invented (in man's own image).

You are a God of life.
Life in freedom is your primary revelation of yourself
and your primary gift to us.
Help us to use it responsibly and protect it at all costs,
even at the expense of a bent regulation now and then.
Amen.

From Psalm 84

How lovely is your dwelling place, O God of the
heavens,
     My soul longs for your presence,
     My heart and soul sing for joy to the living God.

Even the sparrow finds a home
     and the swallow a nest for herself
     where she may lay her young:
     your sacred altars, O God of multitudes. . .

One day in your house is better than a thousand
elsewhere.
     I would rather be a doorkeeper in the house of my God
     than dwell in royal tents of wickedness.
For our God is a sun and a shield
     and honors us with grace and blessing. . . .

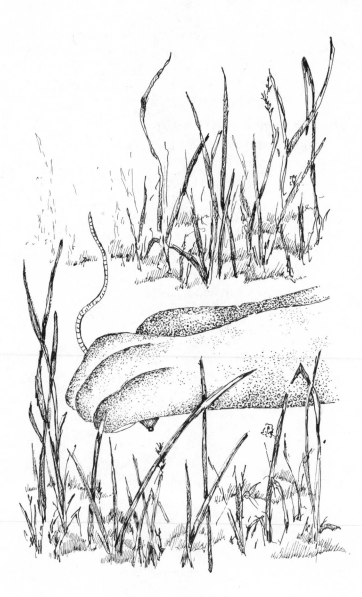

23. The Lion And The Mouse Exchange Favors

A mouse once danced without a look,
Not noticing the road he took.
He suddenly looked down and froze!
He'd danced out on a lion's nose!
　　Zip! Zap! Before he could withdraw
　　He lay beneath the lion's paw.
SORRY! said he in wild dismay—
So Lion let him go his way.

A short time later hunters set
A trap— and Lion fell in their net!
And as he moaned his awful fate
Up came the mouse calm and sedate,
　　And gnawed and gnawed and gnawed and gnawed
　　Until that net in two was sawed!
Then running off their separate ways
They thought: *Yes, kindness always pays.*

Moral: Little friends may prove
to be great friends.

Prayer Before Dancing

Teach us to dance, Creator of this rhythmic world,
Leader of the dance.
We swim in your ocean of rhythm,
rhythm both huge and cosmic, rhythm delicate and
hidden.
Only the numb fail to notice it.
Besides, Creating Spirit,
you gave us human arms and legs
that have the capacity for fluid, rhythmic motion.
We are therefore designed for dancing.

Overwhelmed in joy or sadness, mystification or
bewilderment,
nonetheless (dancers say) *I will go on.*
I will embrace this world's beat and go with it.
I will accept this world, I will dance with its rhythms,
upbeat, downbeat, quick, slow, jubilant, somber.

Spirit Creator,
you fill our bodies with rhythms too:
first the beat of our hearts, then of our breath,
then of our pace and step
then the music we create with voice or fingers.
We notice also, Cosmic Creator,
the massive rhythms of our planet home:
spinning daily from light to darkness,
circling regularly our central Daystar
tipping gracefully in seasonal patterns.
This is the music you have placed us within:
Teach us us to dance.
Amen.

After Psalm 104

Behold on every side, O God, your creatures,
Your countless living things, both great and small,
Your handiwork exquisitely invented,
in wisdom and delight you made them all.

Inhabit they the earth and ocean waters,
With ships above and whales at sport below.,
Each creature looks to you for food in season,
You open up your hand and all things grow.

Things come to life when you breathe forth your Spirit,
in springtime earth will dance in green attire,
The hills will move each time you look upon them,
You touch the mountaintops and they catch fire.

Yes, I will sing to God a song of wonder,
And praise the Spirit of my life in song.
Come, Holy One, and hear my heart's elation,
Rejoicing in your love my whole life long. . . .

24. The Goat and the Lion Decide Not to Fight

One day in the jungle with nothing to eat
And the sun burning down with a terrible heat,
A goat and a lion both tried to be first
As they rushed toward a fountain, near dying of thirst.

Now the goat was youthful and callow and bold
But the lion was proud and haughty and old.
I'm first, said the lion, *This fountain is mine!*
Begone! said the goat, *While I'm feeling benign,*
Or else I will butt you into Kingdom Come!
The lion said: *Goat, you're foolhardy and dumb!*
One bite with my teeth and your young life is through.
Said goat: *Well, just try it, I'll butt you in two!*

Just then they heard feathers, and what did they see?
Three vultures were landing nearby in a tree,
Awaiting the battle where someone would lose,
And they'd get the carcass, they didn't care whose.

So Lion and Goat did a compromise trick:
The one who drinks first will just have to drink quick
They agreed, and in minutes they'd both had enough,
And the frustrated vultures flew off in a HUFF.

Moral: By insisting on your rights
you can forfeit more precious things.

God Most Holy, Alpha and Omega,
God who encompasses all diversity,
human and divine, feminine and masculine,
Spirit who designed the Anemone and the Zebra
and every awesome living thing in between,
Wisdom within and behind the scheduling of the Big
Bang
with all the energies it contained and released,
Loving Strength that gives being to earthquake and
cosmic fire
and inexplicable black holes,
Holy God of the Weird
—by my definition not yours!
—widen my vision, open my heart,
come into my mind as much as possible as you are,
not as I fashion you
to fit my categories.

Take from me my instinctual fear of diversity, of outsiders,
of what seems unacceptably strange.
We never will have enemies if we can only admit
there are really no outsiders in this family—
who have a common story of an unspeakably
awesome past, of connectedness to all that is, a fragile
vulnerability,
and a common heritage of death.

Help me to see diversity as excitement,
revelation and opportunity,
as source of energy,
as a contrasting patch on the colossal quilt of Being.
Amen.

After Psalm 8

God, O God of wonders,
How holy is your name throughout the earth!
    God of stars and thunders,
    How holy is your name throughout the earth!

Behold, our infant children sing your Kyrie,
And make your glory ring above the sky,
    The beauty of the daffodils is eloquent,
    And crickets chant your praises when they cry.

You tower over evil in your majesty,
We look in awe at your night sky above,
    The stars and moon, the magic of your fingertips,
    The Universe, a miracle of love.

You juggle massive stars and giant galaxies,
So, how concerned with humans can you be?
    But you have made us partners in your universe,
    As if like gods and goddesses are we.

The ox and sheep are our responsibility,
And animals and beasts of every size.
    All birds that fly, all fish that swim, rely on us,
    For Earth will die unless we're strong and wise. . . .

25. The Mother Lion Settles an Argument

The animals were arguing
  Which one was the most fertile,
I win, said dog, *I've thirteen pups!*
  I triple that, said turtle.

Then rabbit bragged that nothing matched
  Her rapid reproduction,
But pigs felt sure that they could win
  If they had more instruction.

Next, Algae screamed: *We multiply*
  By geometric fission!
Wait! We'll ask Lioness, said All—
  And go by her decision.

How many whelps have you, they asked,
  Assuming you are tryin'?
I have but one, was her reply,
  But that one is a LION.

Moral: Quantity is no substitute
  for quality.

Prayer to Be Less Competitive

We are mystified—
Elusive Creator Spirit,
invisible as the wind and as free—
with the signals we get from you.

Surely we are not meant to be competitive
the way other animals are
who "naturally"—competitively—battle among
themselves
to determine the most promising individuals to survive
and reproduce.

Among wild animals the strongest is often the most
admired,
but among human animals, another norm prevails—
for you fashioned humans without compelling instincts,
hoping we would choose justice,
learn kindness,
be honored simply to walk humbly alongside of you,
co-responsible co-creators, part of the earth's wondrous
life system.

Quell the hurtful competitiveness
this eccentric culture has instilled in me,
Holy Creator.

Help me freely choose justice, kindness, connectedness
and humility,
whatever the cost.
Amen.

After Psalm 36

This earth is God's with all its wealth,
    this world and those who dwell therein,
for God has set it on the sea,
    and built it on the waters underneath the earth.

Who shall ascend the hill of God?
    Who stand in God's most holy place?
Those with open hands, those with new hearts,
    Those who love the truth and walk in honest caringness.

They will be blest by heaven's care,
    and touch the morning's innocence,
Their searching hearts will look to God
    and seek the face of each elusive Mystery. . . .

26. The Donkey's Shadow Disappears

On a hot sunny day a traveler paid
For a donkey and driver to rent,
But half way to town, when stopping for lunch,
He decided he wasn't content.

I'll eat in the good donkey's shadow, he said,
No, you won't, said his driver and guide,
*You paid for the donkey but not for the shadow
That falls on my good donkey's side.*

Yes, I will! said the man. *No, you won't!* Said the guide.
They shouted like lunatic men.
And the donkey got frightened and ran for the hills,
And never was heard from again.

Moral: In fighting over trifles,
we may lose greater things.

Prayer for Perspective

Bless me with wisdom, my God and my All,
so that in my natural desire to achieve what I prize,
I not overlook more important objectives.

Perspective is often what I lack:
for instance, to see things
from the viewpoint of the common good,
or perhaps a part of your own mysterious
desires for the world.

I will listen for your voice in real events.
They may have something surprising to teach me.

What is the obvious thing that I'm not seeing?
For instance, while we haggle and accumulate,
is our entire planet habitat not under threat?
While we feel bewildered by insoluable problems,
we forget that you are with us and within us.

Bless me with courage enough to choose
what is wise
over what is merely strongly appealing,
to take a long-range view every once in awhile.
Amen.

From Psalm 121

I raise up my eyes to the hills.
    From whence does my help come?
My help comes from the God of my life
    who made the heavens and earth.

God will not let my footing be lost,
    The Compassionate One will not slumber.
Behold, the God who protects the oppressed
    will neither lie down nor sleep.

God is my help, my hope against hope,
    A protection on my right hand.
The sun shall not strike me down by day,
    Nor the moon do me harm by night. . . .

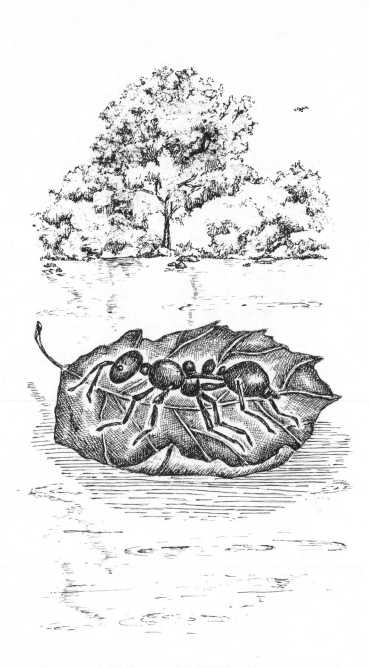

27. The Dove and the Ant Save Each Other

A thirsty ant went down to the lake
To get a drink one day,
But slipped on a patch of slimy mud.
And fell in all the way.

HELP, HELP! he cried, *I'M GOING TO DROWN!*
But a kind dove heard the shout,
And dropped him a leaf of a mulberry bush
Which he used as a boat to get out.

So, tired and worn, when he got to shore,
He heard a hunter's feet
Tip-toeing through the lakeside grass
In search of doves to eat.

TAKE THAT! said ant as he nipped his heel,
OUCH! OUCH! came that hunter's cry,
And the dove heard the racket, jumped from his perch
And disappeared into the sky.

Moral: One good turn
deserves another.

Prayer for Energy

Creator Spirit, when I turn to you,
it is like turning toward the sun—
the massive friendly star that empowers life
on earth.

You empower me,
and you can empower me, I believe,
to achieve all my potential,
all my capacities to grow,
all my dreams of fulfillment
and of usefulness in building a responsible earth
community.

Above all, be present in my potential for love and for
caring,
for responding to each opportunity for small acts of
kindness,
for relieving the burdens of others.

For it is love,
ultimately your love for us and incarnated in us,
that makes the world go around.
Amen.

From Psalm 27

Hear me, Holy One, when I cry aloud,
    by gracious to me and answer me,
For you have said:
    Seek a place before my face.

My heart replies:
    Your face, my God, I do seek,
    Hide not your face from me
For, though my father and mother may forsake me,
    You, Holy One, will take me up.

Teach me your ways, my God,
    and lead me on a level path.
I believe that I shall see the goodness of God
    in the land of life. . . .

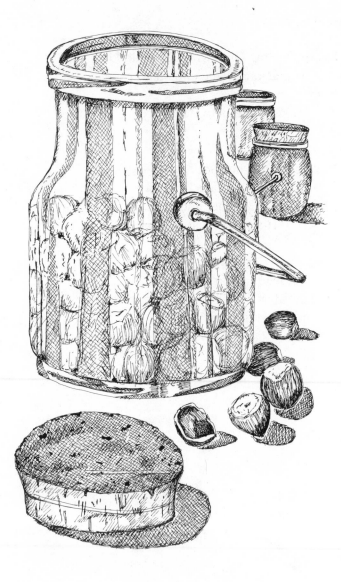

A hungry boy reached reached deep inside
A hazelnut jar in a shop,
But when he tried to pull out his hand,
His fist wouldn't fit through the top.

He screamed and he wailed and he burst into tears,
But the shopkeeper started to sing:
Take a few at a time, sang the patient old man,
And you'll soon have enough for a KING.

Moral: Greed can destroy
opportunity.

Prayer Against Greed

Holy God,
Mystery of Energy within and around us,
you have made us in your own image and likeness—
and so we find ourselves filled with energy,
desires of all kinds,
and yearning for even an eternity of life.

All this drive can, we know, become—
when we separate ourselves from larger concerns—
greed,
that temptation whose epidemic energies, in the form
of world-poluting multinational corporations,
now threaten to destroy life on earth.

We will resist the myth that we can "have it all,"
and the illusion that what we have
defines us.

Save us from ourselves, Holy Wisdom.
Guide us always into the circle of common concern
where solidarity is the new word for salvation.
Amen.

After Psalm 63

O God, you are the God whom I do seek,
For you my body pines, my soul's in pain—
    Like earth herself when parched and deep in dust,
    Like earth herself when rivers long for rain.

Thus have I sought your sanctuary's glow
And feel your awesomeness in all I see,
    For your compassion gives my heart its guide,
    And while I can, my lips shall sing of thee. . . .

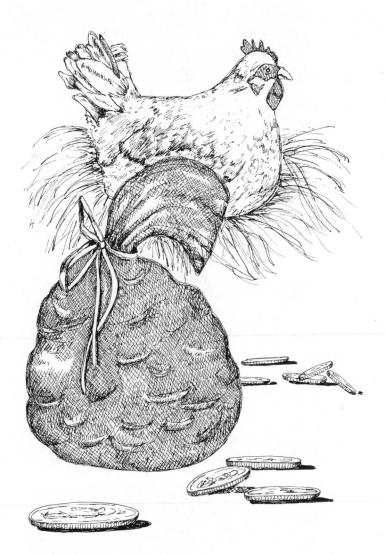

29. The Greedy Woman Overfeeds Her Hen

A woman once owned a perky hen
That laid a fine egg now and then,
    And some she ate and some she sold
    And soon she'd saved a bag of gold.

She thought: *That hen won't eat enough!*
Suppose I feed her sweets and stuff!
    She'll lay huge eggs like we ain't seen,
    And I'll get richer than the QUEEN!

She put her greedy plan to work,
But soon that hen began to shirk,
    Too fat she grew and full of strife,
    And laid no more eggs all her life.

Moral: The urge to exploit the natural world
                    can destroy it.

Is it possible, is it thinkable, True God,
Sacred Mystery within and beneath all that is,
that we might find our way back across the mountains
of time
to the era when our race had more reverence for the
earth
and for living things?
less data and more awe?

Can we recover our connection and companionship
with our earth and its creatures,
and turn away from the focus on weapons and
competitiveness—
to the holiness of pleasure and sexuality,
the primacy of childbirth and nurturance,
with a wise enmity toward isolation, privilege and
wealth?

Above all, can we ever return
to a reverence for the
planet of which we are a part,
using her limited resources with awe and respect?

Connect us again, Holy God,
to our sources of life and liveliness,
and give us new gratitude for our mothering earth,
the energizing rain forest,
and the diversity of living things
that makes possible the life we enjoy,
and reflects so stunningly
your own amazing mystery.
Amen.

From Psalm 148

Bless God from the heavens, bless God in the heights.
    Bless God, all angels, bless God, all living spirits.
Bless God, sun and moon, bless God, shining stars.
    Bless God, you highest heavens,
    and you waters above the heavens. . .

Bless God from the earth, you sea monsters and all
deeps,
    fire and hail, snow and frost,
    stormy wind fulfilling God's command,
    mountains and all hills, fruit trees and all cedars,
    autumn maples, bright and wild,
    oaks that tower, poplars that sway,
    beasts and all cattle,
    creeping things and flying birds:

Bless God. . . .

30. The Tricky Donkey Gets Tricked

A groceryman once bought some salt
And piled it on his donkey's back,
Then started on the long trek home
Along a slippery river track.

    The bags of salt were piled up high
    And felt just like a ton of stones
    Or blocks of granite, clay or lead
    To that poor donkey's aching bones.

Then WHOOPS! his feet slipped! Down he fell
Into the river swirling there,
And all the salt dissolved away—
Which made his load a breeze to bear.

    Next day, again the donkey slipped,
    This time on purpose, thought the man,
    And once again the salt dissolved!
    So that smart grocer made a plan.

He loaded Donkey's aching back
With sponges, piled up high like bricks.
When they got wet, they weighed a ton,
And that cured Donkey of his tricks.

Moral: Don't try the same trick
too many times.

Prayer for the Poor

Why is it, Heart-Inhabiting Wisdom,
that I am so slow to realize
how sweet is the yoke of solidarity with the oppressed,
and how light the burden of compassion for those in
pain?

My shadow-side self tugs me toward that great illusion:
"when I look away, the pain of the poor disappears too."
Or, "you can't really do anything for them: concentrate
on your own spiritual life."

That lightens the burden, of course—but only
temporarily.
The evidence again increases that it is you that dwell in
us all, and that solidarity with them
is our own personal survival as well:
we must learn to join with the needy
in solving our common crisis.

Thus you make the yoke sweet and the burden light
for it is only our own enlivening we seek and demand.

Bless us with this wisdom
and grace us with the courage
to act wisely on it.
Amen.

From Psalm 146

Happy are they whose help is in God,
    The God of Jacob and Rachel,
Who hope in the Spirit, their God and their All,
    The maker of earth and of heaven.

You called the depths of the sea into being,
    And all of the creatures within it,
A God who keeps faith and who saves the oppressed,
    And gives nourishing food to the hungry.

Our God is the one who sets prisoners free
    And opens the eyes of the blinded.
Who raises the heads of those that were crushed,
    And loves the workers of justice. . . .

IV.

History is Written by the Victors

31. A Man Argues With a Wise Lion

A lion and a man, they say,
    were traveling along
When they began to argue who
    was braver and more strong,
Just as their tempers flared to hot,
    they passed a monument
That showed a man killing a lion—
    sculpted in cement.

You see? the man said. *See the truth,*
    the human is the stronger!
My case is closed. I see no need
    to argue any longer!
The lion grinned: *That's made by MEN!*
    Lion sculptors always show
A dozen men held down beneath
    a single lion's toe.

Moral: History is written
    by the victors.

Holy Spirit, infinitely involved in the drama of human
evolution,
you are so close by
as to inhabit every gram and erg of everything that is,
and you are so distant
as to be utterly beyond our grasp.

So close, so distant,
receive at least our awe and wonder,
and our prayer as well that we learn wisdom,
and patience with our own illusions and errors of
judgment.

So much of what humans think they know
turns out to be miniscule and misguided.

What has been human history up to now?
We know not even a hundred thousandth part.
You know it perfectly.

Give us persistence in our spiritual search—
for our world contains the promise
that if we seek, we shall find,
if we knock, it shall be opened—
on a reality exceeding all our expectations.
Amen.

From Psalm 8

O God of every mystery,
　　how majestic is Your name in all the earth,
You whose honor is higher than the sky,
　　Your praise is chanted by the mouths of infants.

You dwell within and around us,
　　and we stand beyond the reach of any enemy.
When I look at the heavens, the work of Your fingers,
　　the moon and the stars which You have established,
　　what is humankind that You are mindful of us,
　　what are earthlings that You can care for us?
Yet You have made us almost divine
　　and crown us with laughter and glory. . . .

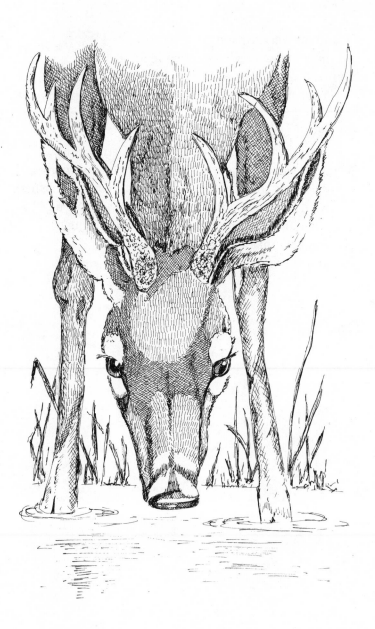

32. The Deer Misjudges His Talents

One summer's day a beautiful deer
    Saw his face in the lake as he drank,
How lovely and strong are my horns, said he,
    But my legs! how skinny and lank!

Just then some hunters and hounds drew near,
    And the legs of the deer raced well,
And he would have escaped—but his horns got caught
    In a branch! With one arrow, he fell.

Moral: Embarrassing things about ourselves
may be our greatest strength.

Prayer for Wisdom

You know well, Holy God,
that I have often thought to myself:
I wish I were differently made—
taller, more athletic, better looking—
with a flashy memory, a resonant voice and perfect
health.

Had I your infinite wisdom, my God,
I suspect I would know better
and appraise more wisely my talents, my strengths and
weaknesses.

Give me enough insight
to be content with all of who I am at the moment,
for I know very incompletely who I am,
and not at all who I shall be.
Amen.

From Psalm 27

The Spirit is my light and my hope,
    whom shall I fear?
The Giver of Life
    is the stronghold of my days.
    Of whom shall I be afraid?

One thing have I asked of our God, that will I seek:
    to dwell at the heart of God's family
    all the days of my life,
    to see before me the divine beauty,
    and cherish God's holy temple.

For God will hide me in the day of trouble,
    and conceal me in perfect care,
    and set me on a safe high place
    where I will sing
    and make melodies of praise. . . .

33. The Dying Farmer Tricks His Sons

A farmer fearing death was near
Summoned his sons so they could hear:
    I fear, my boys, that I'll soon be dead:
    My legacy? Look in the vineyard! he said.

When he died, those sons dug everywhere,
Plowing that vineyard unaware,
    And the vines grew up like never before,
    And the grapes grew plentiful, more and more.

Aha! they said: *Our Pa's estate*
is the lesson that HARD WORK makes life great!
    What a fine legacy for us fools!
    An inheritance richer than money and jewels.

Moral: The best inheritance
is a parent's wisdom.

Prayer for Those Who Look Up to Us

Dear God, why am I stressed out so often trying to
improve people?
What is it that constantly impresses me
with my own spiritual wisdom?
Have I a parasite in my intestines inhabited by the
Angel Gabriel,
biting me periodically with the urge to make divine
announcements?

Have pity, Comforting Spirit, on those who look up to
us.
Make us models of laughter and lightheartedness,
compulsive honesty and persistent self-respect.

If we have any wisdom or virtue others may benefit
from,
let it be hidden beneath good humor and reverence for
life.

Make us good to be around,
and as reticent to bestow on others our unsought advice
as you are yourself.
Amen.

From Psalm 131

O God, I have no utterance,
    my eyes are not raised high,
I do not attempt to unravel mysteries
    too great and too perplexing for me.

Instead I have calmed and quieted my inmost self
    Like an infant quiet at its mother's breast.
Like a child in the comfort of its father's arms,
    I am at peace. . . .

34. The Baby Goat Taunts a Wolf

Way up high on a towering rock
    once climbed a baby goat,
And seeing a wolf far down below,
    she wiggled her shiny white coat.

You can't get me, you slimy wolf,
    with a coat like a filthy rug,
From way up here you look quite queer,
    she mocked,—*And the size of a bug!*

You foolish kid, called out the wolf,
    For making fun of me!
Your only strength is in that rock!
    When you come down you'll see.

Moral: Ridicule is the favorite tool
of weaklings.

Prayer for People J Dislike

Loving God, Mysterious Wind-like Spirit,
blow strongly if you will
and surround with joy all those people whom I dislike.
Be gracious to those whose giftedness I envy.
Bless with wealth and success
those already annoyingly more successful than myself.
They deserve my encouragement, never my scorn.

I pray especially for all those
who do not particularly reverence me,
or may, in fact, dislike me and shun my company.

Give me eyes to see beauty and winsomeness
where I have not seen it before,
and give us all the self confidence to believe
that we would have no enemies at all
if we were known as you, Holy Wisdom, know us.
Amen.

From Psalm 91

Because you have made God your refuge,
    the Most High your safe habitation,
    no evil shall befall you,
    no scourge be ever near your tent.

For God will give the angels charge of you
    to guard you in all your ways,
On their hands they will bear you up
    lest you dash your foot against a stone.

God says: If someone turns to me in love,
    I will deliver them,
    I will protect them, because they know my name.
When anyone calls to me, I will answer them,
    I will be with them in trouble,
    I will rescue them from destruction
        and show them grace and honor. . . .

35. The Pigeons Choose a King

Some nervous pigeons, once upon a time,
Were filled with fear of living on the farm,
    For a hawk would often swoop above their coop
    Where they were hoping to be safe from harm.

Don't be alarmed, that hawk would loudly sing,
It's silly to remain in fear and dread,
Just choose me for your Guardian and King
And you can live in perfect peace instead.

And so the pigeons made the hawk their King,
But soon were filled with TWICE the deep dismay!
    That clever Hawk had failed to make it plain
    That Kings get pigeon dinners every day.

Moral: Some solutions are worse
than the original problem.

Prayer for the Heavily Burdened

There is a striking lack of heroism in my history,
God of Heroes and Martyrs.
There is instead an amazing amount of obvious luck,
and probably even more good fortune I know not of
for there are no doubt physical and pyschic forces
struggling within me—
the forces of healing, for instance,
that have prevented any mortal illness from gaining the
upper hand—
and I have not known of them.

I have not been sucked up into a tornado,
or drowned by a tidal wave,
or struck by lightening:
all strokes of bad luck that have ended the lives of
people around me—
while I live on.
I have never had to live under a tyranical government,
or been duped into giving up my freedom.

While I have shared in physical pain and illness,
I have survived to this day and others have not:
I give thanks.

As for those who must struggle to survive,
I ask to live my days in solidarity with them,
to come to their aid when I can,
to share in their anguish.

I admire their heroism, reluctant as it may have been.
So many of them carry on bravely,
a humbling, inspiring sight.
Amen.

After Psalm 126

May all who weep in the morning,
    planting seeds,
    come back home singing,
    rich in flowers and deeds.

Once God rained good fortune on our tribe,
    And joy like flowers too thrilling to describe:
It was a dream! Our mouth filled up with laughter!
    We couldn't speak, but only shout thereafter.

Then other nations said: their God's a wonder,
    And we adored our God—of flowers and thunder,

Dear God, again send down good days on us—
    Your desert rain can wash out years of dust.
May we who plant in tears—
    go harvesting with cheers. . . .

36. Big Trees Betray the Little Tree

Have you a handle for my ax?
    A woodsman asked the trees,
It's not a lot to ask, said he:
    Which one of you agrees?

The tallest trees decided there
    Was no cause for alarm:
Cut down a lowly ash, they said,
    In that there's little harm.

He did and with the handle fixed,
    He started slashing trees:
Tall oaks, great cedars, maples, birch,
    As many as he'd please.

Too late, the leaders cried in grief,
    Remorseful and perplexed,
Like FOOLS we sacrificed the weak,
    Forgetting we'd be next.

Moral: In the betrayal of the weak
       lies the downfall of tyrants.

Prayer to Be More Cranky

I am much too nice a person, Wild Spirit,
inventor of dinosaurs and earthquakes,
of every cosmic explosion
and of the awesome speed of light,
of intricately formed elements empowered to come alive,
and of living things designed to prey upon each other
and live by hunting and killing.

I am much too nice a person,
much too accommodating—
if I am truly made in your image and likeness.
I am too eager to please,
to fit in everywhere painlessly and unnoticed,
even at the cost of betrayal of my best instincts.

Build in me, Holy One, the courage to fulfill my own
possibilities,
to think my own thoughts,
and risk displeasing people
if it means expressing my best, my truest, self.
Amen.

After Psalm 6

Be gracious to me, O God, I am your child,
　　Heal the despair you hear in my Amen,
Can your love take the turmoil from my soul,
　　And give me total peace within again?

How long before you shall deliver me?
　　How long before you come to save my life?
Because of your great love, I trust in you,
　　Despite my doubts and fears and inner strife. . . .

37. A Mean Dog Nests in the Manger

The meanest dog there ever was
Went looking for a nest
Where he could sleep by day or night
If he should need a rest.

    The horses watched with fearful eyes
    The cruel approaching stranger,
    And sure enough, he went to sleep
    Right in the horses' manger.

How MEAN that creature is, they cried,
To spoil our eating shelf!
He'll snap and bite if we come near,
Yet can't eat straw himself.

Moral: It is heartless to spoil things for others
even though you don't want them yourself.

Prayer to Overcome Mean Feelings

Holy God who knows me as I am,
yes, surely you observe the desert winds of meanness
and envy
that blow through my soul
and stir up the sharp word, the instant judgment, the
closing of my heart.

I am no paragon of virtue,
hardly a saint ripe for veneration.

Rather I am totally human,
sometimes isolated and selfish by choice.
inclined to the whole range of human failings:
egotistical, cowardly, judgmental, careless of human
solidarity,
inclined to meanness and revenge.

I am better than this also,
made in your image in fact,
capable of faithful love, compassion and kindness,
and my very humanness consists in being all this mix
at once.

Make me what you would have me be,
your useful servant despite my ambivalences.
Amen.

From Psalm 17

I call on you, my God, for you will answer,
   Turn your ear to me and hear my words,
Wonderfully show your steadfast care
   For you will save all those who turn to you,

Guard me as the apple of your eye,
   and hide me in the shadow of your wings,
Come hear my prayer, my God, attend my cry,
   Come, give me your compassion in my need. . . .

38. The Selfish Horse Gets an Extra Load

There once was a farm where a donkey and horse
    Had stalls in the barn side by side,
Now the donkey's was dingy and tiny and dark
    But the horse's was sunny and wide.

One day on the road when poor Donkey was ill
    And was feeling already half dead,
He gently asked Horse to take some of his load
    Or this burden will kill me, he said.

O, bunk, said Horse, *I'm a racer supreme,*
    And you donkeys are born with strong backs!
So he pranced up ahead where the master could see,
    But poor Donkey fell dead in his tracks.

So the master removed the poor Donkey's load
    And put it on Horse that day,
Then added the corpse of the Donkey to boot
    Before quickly resuming their way.

And the Horse staggered on but he groaned in his heart
    What a fool I have been! What a jerk!
By refusing to offer to help with the task
    I end up with TWICE as much work.

Moral: Do your part generously,
and you'll avoid worse burdens.

Prayer to Be Less Arrogant

Ultimate Mystery within us and around us,
is there not to be some ultimate forum
in which at last we shall be known as we are,
wherein the people we now ignore or even judge
harshly
will stand beside us in their truth,
a truth that today eludes us?

In that great "Gettin'-up Mornin'"
are the scales finally to fall from our eyes
so we may love as never before
those we do not now know well enough to love?

How totally does our moral judgment of others fail!
What can it be like to be another person,
with different feelings, different hopes, different
memories,
different levels of anxiety, expectation, self-esteem,
hopefulness or despair?
We can never hope to know.

Yet, give us always this desire, Spirit Within.
It will help make our irrepressable arrogance
a little more endurable.
Amen.

From Psalm 31

Into your hands I commend my spirit
　　for You have rescued me, faithful God,
I will rejoice and be glad for your steadfast love.
Because You have seen my affliction,
　　you have taken heed of all my burdens. . .

But still I trust in You, O Holy One,
　　and still I say, You are my God,
　　my times are in your hands.
Let your face shine upon your servant.
　　and save me in your unfailing love. . . .

39. A Boy Cries Wolf

Once there was a foolish boy
Whose job it was to guard some sheep
    In case a hungry wolf might come
    To pounce upon them in their sleep.

The owners told him: *If a wolf*
Should come, be sure to give a cry
    So we can come and save the sheep
    And give that wolf a swift goodbye.

The foolish boy grew bored one night,
And cried out *Wolf! Wolf!* just for jokes,
    And farmers came from far and wide,
    But left disgusted by his hoax.

But then at midnight that boy spied
A savage wolf about to strike,
    WOLF! WOLF! he screamed, but no one came
    And sheep and shepherd died alike.

Moral: Those who enjoy
making fools of others
often make fools of themselves.

Prayer Not to Make a Fool of Myself

Holy God,
I am terrified when I observe the foolishness within
and around me,
and all the frightful limitations of the human mind and
heart
and especially the cruelty in human nature
that would make fools of those too quick to trust.

Give me the wisdom not to make a fool of myself
or anyone else.

Yet my illusions are foolish.
Do I not look a little foolish at times to your all-seeing
eye?
A walking clown maybe, a bit of a buffoon, a mild joke?

I hope—and trust—you enjoy, Holy One,
the prodigious circus you have created on the face of
the earth.
Amen.

After Psalm 23

God shepherds me,
    I shall not want at all,
I'm led to find a resting place
    where the grass is green and tall.

I'm shepherded to rest
    beside clear water still as glass,
Where my drink is fresh and cold
    and all my thirst shall pass.

Although I roam
    through valleys dark with death,
I have no fear for you are here
    as near as blood and breath.

Your rod, your staff, your step, your silence,
    each will comfort me,
Good Shepherd! Good Shepherdess!
    You're everything to me.

You cook us food
    and we forget our woes,
You rub sweet oil into our hair,
    our wine cup overflows.

Then feeling full and free to roam
    or sleep beneath the sun,
Your goodness still shepherds us
    until the day is done. . . .

40. The Fox Outwits the Crow

One day a young crow snatched a fat piece of cheese
From the porch of a house made of stone,
Then she flew to the top of a Juniper Tree
To enjoy her good fortune alone.

But a fox passing by got a whiff of the cheese,
The best of his favorite hors d'oeuvres,
So he called to the crow, *Hey, you glamorous thing,*
Does your voice match your beautiful curves?

The crow was so pleased by the flattering words
She quickly took out a libretto,
How fondly that fox will listen, she thought,
To hear how I caw in falsetto.

She opened her mouth—and the cheese tumbled out,
Which the fox gobbled up full of malice
While he chuckled to think how that dim-witted crow
Could believe she was MARIA CALLAS.

Moral: Attending to flattery
comes at a high price.

Prayer Against Vanity

Holy Wisdom, my Creator and Friend,
give me a serene and inspired view of myself,
so that neither the winds of disapproval
darken the depths of my soul
nor the approval of others
mean too much to me.

Grant me a lightheartedness that defeats vanity,
loving compassion based in healthy self-esteem,
and an honest humility without pretense.

In you I was created with all my gifts and limitations.
In you I live and move and have my splendid being.
In your love and support I will become more fully
who you meant me to be.
Amen.

From Psalm 90

O God, you have been home to us for many
generations,
    since long before even the mountains were born,
    long before you formed the earth and the world,
You are God. . .

In your eyes, a thousand earthly years pass as did
yesterday,
    or as one watch of the night. . .
Our years come to only seventy or so, if we're blessed,
    and even reach eighty for the strong. . .

Teach us, O God, so to number our days,
    that we may have a heart of wisdom. . . .